THE PICTORIAL HISTORY OF
ST. GILES'
CATHEDRAL

 THE HIGH KIRK   OF EDINBURGH

ST. GILES' CATHEDRAL

THE HIGH KIRK OF EDINBURGH

BY THE VERY REV. H. C. WHITLEY Ph.D., D.D.
Dean of the Thistle

ST. GILES' is the very heart of Scotland. Its stones speak our strenuous history.

In 854 there was a church of some kind on this site on the spiny ridge of Edinburgh. It belonged to Lindisfarne (Holy Isle), where Columba's monks had first brought the Gospel from Iona. In 1150, the monks of St. Giles' were farming lands round about, and a bigger church was built in that century. That this first parish church of Edinburgh was dedicated to St. Giles', a saint popular in France, was probably due to the Auld Alliance of Scotland and France against the common enemy of England.

In 1243, because Cardinal Otto from Rome found many Scottish churches in use without proper dedication, David de Bernham, Bishop of St. Andrews, duly dedicated St. Giles'. The Bishop's book of Devotions, with his note on the fly-leaf, is in a library in Paris.

Froissart tells that French chevaliers and Scots lords met secretly in St. Giles' to plan a raid into England. The following year, 1385, the English King Richard II led one in return into Scotland and burnt the abbeys of Melrose, Dryburgh and the church of St. Giles'. All that is certainly left of the ancient church are the four massive central pillars. During the nineteenth-century restoration the scarring of fire was found on these.

Almost at once, the King and townsfolk gave grants of land towards the rebuilding of the church, which was now to be 'thatched with stone'. A contract was given out for five chapels to be built in 'masonlike' manner: the remains of three of these are incorporated in what is now called the Moray Aisle Chapel. In 1409 was built what is now the best preserved corner of St. Giles', the Albany Aisle. It was originally two chapels, presented by the Duke of Albany

The Statue of John Knox. This great Scottish Reformer's influence extended far beyond the bounds of Edinburgh.

and his associate, the Earl of Douglas; it is said, either in expiation for the murder of the Duke's nephew, heir to the throne, or in thanksgiving for their acquittal of the charge.

In 1416, during a lull in the rebuilding, storks nested on St. Giles'.

In 1436 there was a solemn mass for the soul of the murdered King, James I, with 50s. worth of white wax candles.

During the following years the "Vicars of St. Giles'" were often sent abroad to the English and French courts. In 1448 the Vicar was sent to choose a French bride for the young Scottish King, James II. He brought back Mary of Gueldres; and next year he was sent again 'to seek, exact and receive' her dowry, 'or part thereof'.

The ambition of every medieval church was realised for St. Giles' in 1454, when Preston of Gorton made a free gift of a precious relic. This was the arm-bone of St. Giles, which he had secured at much trouble and expense in France. It was mounted in gold, with a diamond ring on its finger; and an aisle was built in Preston's memory by the Town Council. It is now the Preston Aisle, and a carving of his arms—three unicorn heads—is still visible on a boss of the roof.

In 1460, after the death of James II due to a bursting cannon, his widowed Queen took to building. To this period is due the lengthening of the Choir to the East, forming the Chancel; the heightening of the roof, and the clerestory windows. Also the graceful 'King's Pillar' on the North side of the church, which bears her arms, the King's, a prince's shield and the fleur-de-lys of France. In the first two shields the tressure is incomplete, to show the King's death and her widowhood.

St. Giles' was growing in importance as well as in size, and in 1467 a Papal Bull confirmed James III's proposal that it should become a Collegiate Church. The enlarging and enriching of the building continued. Guild money, ship-dues and fines all went 'to the kirk werk'. The Merchants of Edinburgh had their own Chapel of the Holy Blude, of which they formed a Confraternity. The wine merchants shipping between France and Leith (and still using today the old monastic vaults) had their own chapel to St. Anthony.

FACING PAGE: *The Nave, looking East.*

 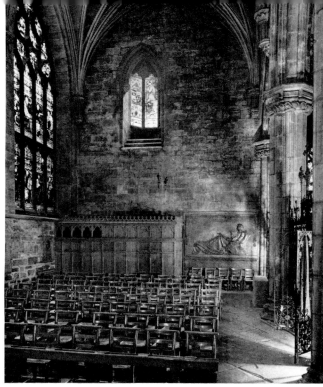

ABOVE, *left:* View of the South Aisle, facing West. On the pillars hang banners of famous Scottish regiments. The railings on the left screen the Moray Aisle. *Right:* The Moray Aisle Chapel, looking West towards the doorway installed for the use of the Court of Session, with the Stevenson memorial alongside, and an oriel window above. FACING PAGE: The Moray Aisle, facing East. The canopied pulpit was erected in 1884 to mark the resumption of the Daily Service after a lapse of 200 years. Beyond the screen is the arched doorway leading to the Ante-Chapel of the Thistle Chapel.

THE 'BANNER OF THE HOLY GHOST'

The Masons and Wrights received the Chapel of St. John in 1475.

In 1496 the Hammermen (smiths) took over the chapel of St. Eloi, of which there are still traces on the North wall. It had a window with their badge of an elephant. They hung here the 'Blue Blanket', the 'Banner of the Holy Ghost'—an old flag which is said to have been brought from the Holy Land by Scots Crusaders, and later to have been carried at Flodden. After Mary Queen of Scots' defeat with Bothwell, it was carried in front of her in the High Street to keep the mob from attacking her. The Guilds took it from St. Giles' at the Reformation and keep it still. It hangs now in the Trades Maidens' Hospital.

In 1474, an English dowry was paid down on the High Altar of St. Giles' for a daughter of Edward IV, but the alliance with James IV did not come off and the money was repaid in full.

In 1488 James III was assassinated, and James IV, greatest of the Stewarts, came to the throne. It was during this century that the

The memorial to Robert Louis Stevenson, novelist and poet of world-wide reputation. Born in Edinburgh in 1850 he died in Samoa in 1894.

Crown steeple of St. Giles', known the world over, was built. The King loved learning; when his friend Chepman brought printing to Scotland in 1508, the King took a personal interest in the work. He presented the poet Gavin Douglas to St. Giles'. In August 1513 Douglas was finishing his translation of Virgil's *Aeneid* into Scots, and Chepman was seeing the completion of the Chapel to St. John which he had built and endowed in St. Giles' (now the Chepman Aisle). There was provision for a priest, who was to take no part 'in games of chance'. The arms of Chepman and his wife are still visible, carved in stone; and also the eagle, sign of the Evangelist, holding a scroll with '*In principio—*' the opening words of St. John's Gospel, 'In the beginning was the Word'. This was also Chepman's trademark. The French Queen had sent King James a ring, begging him to take 'but three steps into English

Continued on page 6

ABOVE, *left:* This memorial to the Regent Moray is in the Moray Aisle Chapel on the South side of the Cathedral. The bronze tablet was taken from the original tomb. The window above shows John Knox conducting the funeral of "the good Earl". RIGHT: The South Transept, with the organ and the University stalls. FACING PAGE: A long view of the North Transept, showing Dr. Strachan's window beyond the carved stone screen. Banners and battle honours of famous regiments and squadrons are mounted on the pillars.

THE SLAUGHTER OF FLODDEN FIELD

ground' if young Henry VIII of England—James' brother-in-law—should attack France, and one of the King's last acts before marching with a great army was to attend the dedication of Chepman's Chapel in St. Giles'.

Four weeks later St. Giles' was again crowded, this time with women and children weeping for the men killed in the terrible slaughter of Flodden Field: 'The Flowers o' the Forest' were 'a' wede awa'.

After Flodden, Church as well as State decayed. In St. Giles', greed possessed the clergy: chapels increased and worship degenerated. In all, there were now about 50 altars crowded in, each with its images and candles. The greatest image was that of St. Giles', carved in wood, but far from showing him as an old hermit who lived on roots and the milk of his tame hind, the image was gorgeously dressed in velvet and jewels, and freshly gilded each year at the expense of the Town.

Money-making and ignorance beset the whole Roman Church at this time, as witnessed Luther. It was priests who began the Reformation in Scotland, and were among the first martyrs. After two men were burnt alive in Edinburgh in 1534, two priests of St. Giles' fled 'for heresy'. Bibles in English were publicly burnt; but offerings to images sharply declined.

In 1555 John Knox came secretly back from Geneva, and lodged in the High Street, where people flocked to hear him. For almost a year he moved about Scotland, preaching and giving to the people the Sacrament of the Lord's Supper, where all sat equally together, passing the Common Cup and Common Bread from hand to hand. Then, being called to Geneva and having made no headway with Mary de Guise, the Queen Regent, (mother of Mary Queen of Scots) he left again.

But the people were roused. Next St. Giles' Day, September 1st, the great image was brought out to be processed through the Town. This had become an almost pagan occasion, with garlands of flowers, a live bull, bagpipes and mummers. The crowd broke up the procession, threw the image into the Nor' Loch which lay below the castle, and later fished it out and burnt it. Next year the clergy applied to the Town for a replacement, but the City Fathers replied that while it was commanded in Holy Writ to cast down images, where it was commanded to replace them at public expense 'they had nocht read'.

Next year, 1559, the Queen Regent, with her French army, opposed

Continued on page 10

THE PRESTON AISLE

LEFT: Looking towards the Preston Aisle from the Choir. In the background is the Royal Pew, and round it the stalls of the Royal Household. ABOVE: A capital in the Preston Aisle. The three unicorns on a shield are the arms of William Preston of Gorton who, in 1454, procured and presented to the Cathedral an arm bone of St. Giles. BELOW: A part of the roof of the Preston Aisle. On the centre boss are the three towers of the coat of arms of the City of Edinburgh. The Preston arms are on the boss, *centre left*.

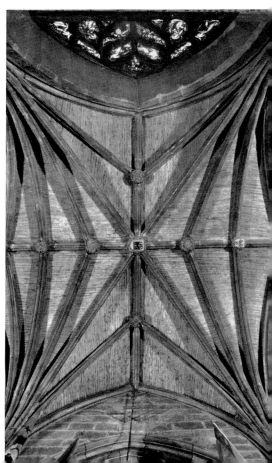

THE CHEPMAN AISLE AND MONTROSE MEMORIAL

ABOVE: The Preston Aisle looking East towards the door of the Thistle Chapel. The Royal Pew is on the right. Set into the wall is the oldest-known representation of the coat of arms of the City of Edinburgh. RIGHT: The Chepman Aisle and the monument to James Graham, Marquis of Montrose, illustrious Captain-General of the forces raised in Scotland for the King's service. He was executed in 1650. BELOW: Detail of the Montrose monument, erected in 1888 by the Clan Graeme.

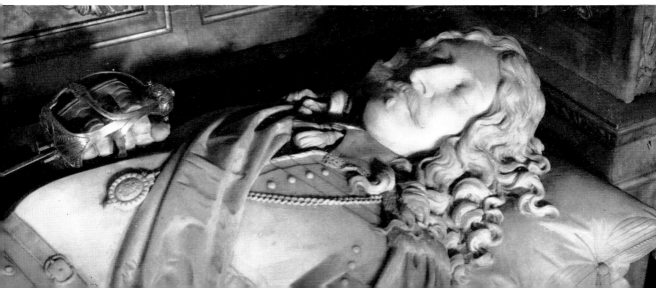

THE ROYAL PEW

ABOVE: The Royal Pew, showing the stalls of The Queen and the Duke of Edinburgh. In front are the stalls of Lord Lyon and his Court. LEFT: The Ante-Chapel to the Thistle Chapel. Built in 1911, to the design of Sir Robert Lorimer, this replaces the ruined Chapel Royal at Holyrood. The names on the wall are those of former Knights of this ancient Order, founded about 1470 by James VI.

A GREAT PUBLIC THANKSGIVING IN 1560

the Reformers at Perth; and Knox hurried back to join them. They defeated her and swept triumphant into Edinburgh, with Lord James Stewart, later Regent Moray, at their head; and on 1st July Knox preached for the first time in St. Giles'. In three weeks they were driven out, but a preacher called Willock stayed in St. Giles' although French soldiers in scarlet cloaks and gilt morions clattered up and down to drown his voice.

In October the Reformers were back, and Knox preached on Psalm 80: 'Give ear, O Shepherd of Israel'. The Queen Regent was in Leith, and scaling-ladders to attack that town were made in St. Giles' 'which not a little grieved the preachers'. In November she drove them out again, and St. Giles' was re-consecrated with holy water. In these dark days of defeat, Knox was the 'one voice' to whom all rallied.

In March 1560 a peaceful English army for the first time crossed the Border, joined with the Reformers and forced the French to evacuate Scotland. On July 19th Knox preached at a great public thanksgiving in St. Giles', and in August was produced the Church's Book of Order, with its emphasis on the Lord's Table, and baptism in face of the congregation; the last mass had been said in St. Giles'.

The following March saw the first great Communion Service in St. Giles'. By now it had been swept clear of all altars and images, and whitewashed: long tables spread with bleached linen were fenced off, and on the benches sat all those, rich and poor, who could answer for their Faith—'in great decency and very good order', wrote Randolph, the English envoy.

That very summer, Mary Queen of Scots landed at Leith. She never went to St. Giles' except to that division called the Tolbooth where she opened Parliament with 'a very pretty speech'. But five times she summoned Knox, to try to win him, or to scold him. After he preached against her proposed marriage to Philip of Spain's son, she could hardly speak for tears of rage and 'womanly owling'. Her banns of marriage to Darnley were cried there, and he came once to sit in the Royal seat, but resented the sermon bitterly.

In 1562 Knox officiated at the wedding of James Stewart to the Earl of Mar's daughter, 'after long love'. The couple went down the Royal Mile to Holyrood, where Mary gave them a great banquet. Eight years later the murdered corpse of James, now Regent Moray, was borne up from Holyrood Chapel to St. Giles' in magnificent procession —the royal pennant carried in front. Knox preached his friend's funeral

Continued on page 14

Page 10

THE ROOF OF THE THISTLE CHAPEL

TOP, *left:* Detail of the roof of the Ante-Chapel. LEFT: Detail of the roof of the Thistle Chapel. The carving, picked out in gold and colour, is remarkably fine. ABOVE: A wide view of the roof of the Chapel. The centre boss shows St. Andrew with the saltire cross, and another the pelican, the symbol of piety. Angels support Scottish coats of arms, and play upon musical instruments.

THE THISTLE CHAPEL

The Thistle Chapel was built by John David, 12th Earl of Leven and 11th Earl of Melville, and his brothers, in fulfilment of their father's wish to restore the ruined Chapel Royal at the Palace of Holyroodhouse. This was found to be impossible, so the new Chapel was built in St. Giles'; the most ornate building of its kind to be erected in Scotland since the Middle Ages. The Order of the Thistle is the most ancient Order of Chivalry in Scotland, and the Knights' stalls, ranged around the walls, carry the arms of many famous Scotsmen, past and present members of the Order. The star of the Order, a St. Andrew's Cross, is shown above.

THE PHOTOGRAPHS

CENTRE: The Thistle Chapel, looking towards the Holy Table. BELOW: The stalls on the North side of the Chapel, and the door leading from the Ante-Chapel. TOP, *right*: Detail of the Royal coat of arms on The Queen's stall. BOTTOM, *right*: The Queen's stall; the Royal arms are carved on the front and those of Queen Anne are on the side.

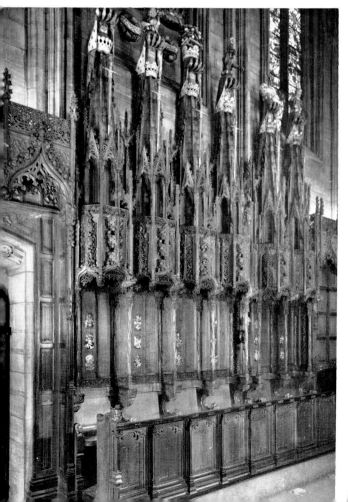

THE EAST DOOR AND THE OLD STONE

LEFT: The East door; fourteenth-century workmanship. ABOVE: Carving of the coat of arms of the City of Edinburgh. This old stone, now set into the East wall of the Preston Aisle, was discovered during the restoration by Chambers of 1872-83.

THE NATIONAL COVENANT

sermon, and he is buried below what has ever since been called the Moray Aisle. The memorial brass by Buchanan luckily survives.

Another brass tablet, of a dog carrying a purse, tells of John Craig, Knox's assistant at this time. The dog, which saved him as he fled through Italy, accompanied him to Scotland. In June 1566 there was a thanksgiving service for Mary's son; eight months later, the explosion of Kirk o' Field; and eight weeks later Craig cried the banns of her marriage to Bothwell, calling heaven and earth to witness his strongest disapproval as he did so.

Mary abdicated, but a Queen's party fought on and mounted cannon on the roof of St. Giles' to fire on the castle. Knox was exiled to St. Andrews, but brought back, a dying man, in 1572. He inducted his successor, Lawson, died in his High Street Manse, and is buried in the graveyard at the back of St. Giles'. His grave, like his life, is humble. 'Here lies one', it was said, 'who neither feared nor flattered any flesh'.

The struggle against England, France and the Papacy was over: that with Kings and Bishops had begun. Mary's son, James VI (and I), appreciated the threat to absolute power of a democratic Church. He strove hard to introduce Episcopacy, with himself as Head of the Church. When a minister attacked Bishops from the pulpit, he answered him back warmly from the Royal chair. Twice he exiled the ministers for their outspokenness; and Lawson died in poverty in London. There was one happy occasion when the minister, Robert Bruce, crowned Ann of Denmark in Holyrood, and she came in progress up to St. Giles' and sat in the East End 'under a fair canopy of velvet'. There were flowers strewn everywhere, and wine 'for all strangers'. But by the end of James' reign there were Bishops in the pulpit, the Table suppressed in favour of kneeling; the building was cut into three and the steeple used as a prison.

James' son, Charles I, was crowned in Holyrood in June, 1633, and came to St. Giles', where instantly, Anglican clergy in full dress took over, using the Anglican prayer book. It was he who made Edinburgh a Bishopric, and St. Giles' a Cathedral. It caused bitter feeling. When in the first full service the Bishop called upon Dean Hanna to read the Collect, a Luckenbooth wifie, Jenny Geddes, cried out: 'De'il colic the wame o' ye!' and hurled her stool at him. The rebellion she sparked off eventually carried away both throne and Church in England. The National Covenant was drawn up in 1638, and there is in the Chepman Aisle an original copy of it, signed at Linlithgow.

In August, 1639, the first Lord High Commissioner walked in procession up the Royal Mile to represent Royalty at the General Assembly: a tradition happily perpetuated. When Charles returned to St. Giles' in 1641 it was to a Presbyterian service. There was an agreement signed in St. Giles' for a United Presbyterian Church of Scotland and England, but, later, when the

Continued on page 18

THE COMMUNION TABLE

The Communion Table is of light oak, elaborately carved, coloured and gilded. In the centre is the Paschal Lamb, and on either side winged figures supporting shields bearing the emblems of the Passion. St. Giles with his hind appears in the centre panel on the East side, and emblems of the Evangelists at either end. The reredos was presented by the Merchant Company, to mark the National Service of Thanksgiving and Dedication held in St. Giles' Cathedral in 1953 shortly after Queen Elizabeth's Coronation in Westminster Abbey, and is the work of Mr. Esme Gordon.

NORTH SIDE OF THE CHANCEL
BELOW: North side of the Chancel, showing the King's Pillar and the Moderator's stall, presented to mark the Moderatorial Year (1913–14) of Dr. Andrew Wallace Williamson, Minister of St. Giles' from 1910 to 1925.

THE CHOIR, FACING WEST
BELOW: The Choir and Nave, facing West, showing the stall of the Dean of the Thistle and the Chapel Royal, with his banner displayed on the pillar above. On the painted board above the arch are the arms of George III.

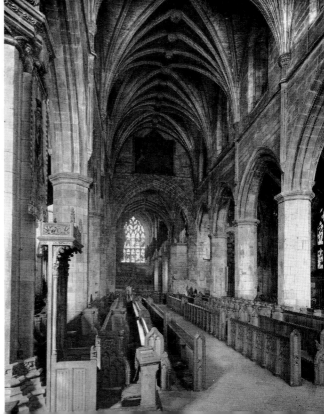

THE CHANCEL

ABOVE: The roof of the Chancel. In 1460 the roof of the Chancel was raised, and the clerestory windows shown in this photograph were added. LEFT: Details of the King's Pillar (above the Moderator's stall) showing two of the shields on the capital. The lion rampant is the coat of arms of James II, to the left of the photograph are the arms of his wife, Mary of Gueldres, and on the East side the lion rampant with a label of three points denotes their son, later James III. The fourth shield carries the fleur-de-lys of France. These carvings probably date from about 1460—the year of James II's death. This pillar and the one opposite were erected when the church was rebuilt and enlarged after the fire of 1385.

* * *

THE CHOIR

FACING PAGE: The Choir, showing the pulpit and lectern. The pulpit, carved in Caen stone, is the work of John Rhind, and the six panels in high relief depict the six Acts of Mercy. The Sacrament of Baptism is dispensed here. In the foreground are the Choir stalls.

THE CHAMBERS AISLE

The Chambers Aisle, the Chapel of Youth. In 1927 this Aisle, named in honour of St. Giles' great benefactor, William Chambers, Lord Provost of Edinburgh, was set aside as a Chapel of Youth. The Colours of the Youth Organisations of Edinburgh hang here, and, attached to the North wall, is a baptismal font. The original furniture and fittings were designed by Sir Robert Lorimer. The Nativity scene, carved in low relief, is the work of Mr. and Mrs. Meredith Williams.

CROMWELL'S REGIME

Scottish forces were defeated, this was abandoned.

After their victory at Dunbar, Cromwell's men used part of St. Giles' for their 'exercise in religion'. 'Captains, commandos, troopers . . . entered the pulpit with their swords hung by their sides, and some carrying pistols . . .' They abolished 'the day called Christmas', the Royal chair and the Assembly. There was no Sacrament for six years, and St. Giles' was cut into four.

At the Restoration there was a general thanksgiving, and a bonfire at the Cross, into which Jenny Geddes, 'Princess of the Tron', threw 'her creels, baskets and cutty stool . .' The Royal chair was restored. The spiked head and broken remains of the great Marquis of Montrose were gathered together, and given magnificent burial in the Chepman Aisle, where his memorial is. Only his heart, now believed to be in America, is still missing.

Disappointment followed. Parliament met in a part of St. Giles' under a King's Commissioner, and restored Episcopacy. In 1664 Covenanters were caught at Rullion Green by 'bluidy Dalzell'—Tam Dalzell of the Binns—and imprisoned with cruelty in 'Haddo's Hole' above the North porch. (This cell was called after Graham of Haddo, a condemned Royalist, once imprisoned there.) Only Wyshart, Montrose's Chaplain and now Bishop, brought them food and drink. They were tortured and hanged, and the 'Killing Times' continued. The Marquis of Argyll, Montrose's old enemy, was beheaded, and his head stuck on a pike on the East gable. But his monument, too, is in St. Giles'.

At last, in 1685, the Royal chair was once more draped in black for the death of Charles II. After three years of James VII and II, William of Orange landed in England, accompanied, among others, by the

Continued on page 24

* * •

THE NORTH SIDE OF THE CHOIR

FACING PAGE: *The North side of the Choir, showing the stalls of the Dean of the Thistle and the Moderator, with the King's Pillar behind. The two octagonal pillars (centre) date from about 1120. The steps are of Greek marble.*

Page 18

THE NORTH TRANSEPT

ABOVE: The North Transept, showing the crossing. The organ loft is above the stone screen: the door in the screen leads to a porch and thence into the High Street. To the East is the Choir and one of the original octagonal pillars.

THE ARGYLL MEMORIAL

FACING PAGE: Bay on North side of the Nave sometimes called St. Eloi's Chapel or the Hammermen's Chapel, in honour of the Craft that endowed it. In the West wall is a romanesque cap, found during Chambers' restoration.

THE ARGYLL MEMORIAL

LEFT and BELOW: This magnificent memorial to the eighth Earl and first Marquis of Argyll was erected in the North Bay at the suggestion of Queen Victoria. Argyll, the man chiefly responsible for the execution of the Marquis of Montrose (commemorated on the South side of the Cathedral) was himself executed at the Mercat Cross outside St. Giles'. The floor of the bay is of Irish marble, inlaid with a mosaic of encaustic tiles. The medallions represent the lion of St. Mark and the eagle, symbol of St. John. The window behind—the Argyll Window—carries the coats of arms of the great Covenanting leaders—Sutherland, Cassilis, Lothian, Balmerino, Argyll, Dalhousie, Loudoun, Eglinton, Leven, Sir Thomas Hope, Lord Newark, and Johnston of Warriston. This fine window was made by the Glass Stainers' Company of Glasgow.

* * *

THE WEST END OF THE NORTH AISLE

FACING PAGE: The North Aisle, looking West. The window in the West wall is by William Morris, designed by Burne Jones, and commemorates Lord Curriehill. The slender pillar on the right of the photograph is known as the Albany Pillar—taking its name from Robert, Duke of Albany, second son of King Robert II. The wrought iron rails screen the Albany Aisle.

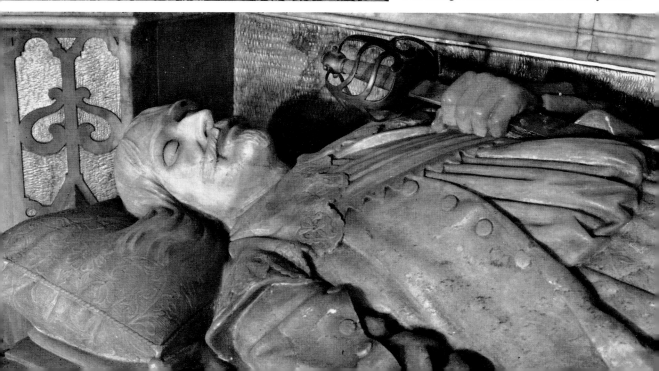

THE ALBANY AISLE

LEFT and ABOVE: The Albany Aisle, now the War Memorial Chapel, dedicated on St. Andrew's Day, 1951, in the presence of the Knights of the Thistle. The perpetually burning Lamp of Remembrance was lit by Admiral of the Fleet Viscount Cunningham of Hyndhope. The panels carved between the arms of the Cross represent the elements, fire, air, water and earth.
BACK COVER: The Cathedral from the South East. In the foreground is the Thistle Chapel, and, behind, the Crown Tower.

THE GREAT WORK OF WILLIAM CHAMBERS

exiled Scottish preacher, William Carstares. On one of the great pillars is the memorial to this scholar, statesman and minister of St. Giles'. When the Union of Parliaments was achieved in 1707, and consecrated by a service in St. Giles', it was Carstares who secured the independence of the Church of Scotland, while achieving that 'perpetual concord betwixt the two realms' for which Knox in times past had 'long looked'.

Quieter times succeeded. In 1736 a condemned smuggler, escaping from his funeral sermon, caused the Porteous Riot, so vividly described by Sir Walter Scott. In 1745, a meeting was hastily convened in St. Giles' to decide whether the Town would admit or resist Prince Charles Edward and his Highlanders, when a messenger entered and presented a courteous personal letter signed 'Charles, Prince of Wales', and the meeting hastily dispersed.

Daniel Defoe visited St. Giles' in 1727. Whitfield preached there. The great preacher, Dr. Hugh Blair, was admired both by Dr. Johnson and by Robert Burns. A very welcome visitor was King George IV, in 1827 the first occupant of the Royal pew for almost 200 years.

This visit was followed by a period of reconstruction described by Dr. Cameron Lees as 'disastrous'. St. Giles' was only saved for us by the devoted and generous care of William Chambers, Lord Provost of Edinburgh, to whom we owe the single and seemly Kirk of today. His great work was completed in 1883.

The Thistle Chapel was begun in 1909, and inaugurated in 1911. The donors, the Earl of Leven and his brothers, had hoped to restore the Chapel of Holyrood, but this, unfortunately, proved impracticable. The Thistle Chapel is attached to the South East corner of St. Giles' and used for the services of the Most Ancient and Most Noble Order of the Thistle, originally founded by James III. Near it, in the Preston Aisle, is the present day Royal Pew.

So, after more than a thousand years, St. Giles' is still a living parish church: the 'Townes Kirk'; a National Shrine and the hospitable home of the Scottish spirit.

ACKNOWLEDGMENTS

The publishers are most grateful to the Moderator and Kirk Session of St. Giles' Cathedral for permission to produce this book. All the photographs were taken by A. F. Kersting, A.I.I.P., F.R.P.S., with the exception of those on pages 3, 4, 5, 7, 8 (left), 17, 20 and 23 which were taken by Norward Inglis, and the front cover, taken by A. L. Hunter.

SBN 85372 019 3   1173/10